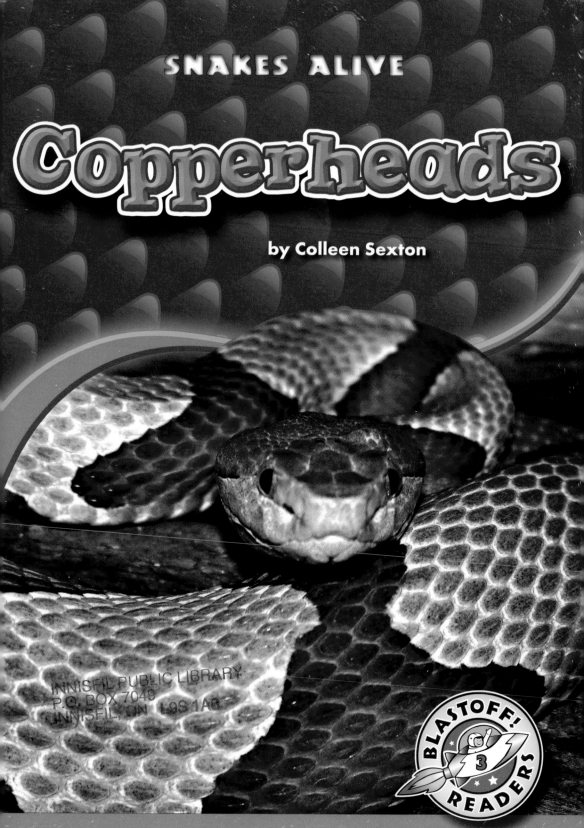

SNAKES ALIVE

Copperheads

by Colleen Sexton

BELLWETHER MEDIA • MINNEAPOLIS, MN

BLASTOFF!
3
READERS

Note to Librarians, Teachers, and Parents:

Blastoff! Readers are carefully developed by literacy experts and combine standards-based content with developmentally appropriate text.

Level 1 provides the most support through repetition of high-frequency words, light text, predictable sentence patterns, and strong visual support.

Level 2 offers early readers a bit more challenge through varied simple sentences, increased text load, and less repetition of high-frequency words.

Level 3 advances early-fluent readers toward fluency through increased text and concept load, less reliance on visuals, longer sentences, and more literary language.

Level 4 builds reading stamina by providing more text per page, increased use of punctuation, greater variation in sentence patterns, and increasingly challenging vocabulary.

Level 5 encourages children to move from "learning to read" to "reading to learn" by providing even more text, varied writing styles, and less familiar topics.

Whichever book is right for your reader, Blastoff! Readers are the perfect books to build confidence and encourage a love of reading that will last a lifetime!

This edition first published in 2011 by Bellwether Media, Inc.

No part of this publication may be reproduced in whole or in part without written permission of the publisher. For information regarding permission, write to Bellwether Media, Inc., Attention: Permissions Department, 5357 Penn Avenue South, Minneapolis, MN 55419.

Library of Congress Cataloging-in-Publication Data

Sexton, Colleen A., 1967-
Copperheads / by Colleen Sexton.
    p. cm. – (Blastoff! readers: Snakes alive)
Includes bibliographical references and index.
Summary: "Simple text and full-color photography introduce beginning readers to copperheads. Developed by literacy experts for students in kindergarten through third grade"–Provided by publisher.
ISBN 978-1-60014-453-0 (hardcover : alk. paper)
1. Copperhead–Juvenile literature. I. Title.
QL666.O69S484 2010
597.96'3–dc22   20100007

Text copyright © 2011 by Bellwether Media, Inc.
Printed in the United States of America, North Mankato, MN.

080110   1162

Contents

Copperheads are **poisonous** snakes named for the red-brown color on their heads.

They have flat, triangle-shaped heads with turned-up **snouts**.

Copperheads have narrow necks and thick bodies.

Their dry skin has tough **scales**. The scales cover and protect their bodies.

Most copperheads grow 20 to 36 inches (51 to 91 centimeters) long.

Copperheads grow throughout their lives. They **shed** their outer skin when it gets too tight.

Copperheads have brown or tan bodies with gray, tan, or orange markings.

The markings are shaped like hourglasses. They are narrow on the snake's back and belly and wide on its sides.

The colors and markings are **camouflage**. They help copperheads match rocks, dead leaves, and other surroundings.

= areas where copperheads live

Copperheads live
in the eastern and
central United
States. They find
cover in rocky
hillsides, woods,
and tall grasses.

13

Copperheads
need to hide
from **predators**.
Hawks, opossums,
and other snakes
hunt copperheads.

Sometimes copperheads shake their tails in dead leaves to make a rattling sound. The sound is a warning to stay away!

copperhead prey

Copperheads stay still in their hiding places when they hunt. They wait for birds, frogs, mice, and other **prey** to pass by.

Young copperheads have a yellow tip on their tails. The snakes stay still and wiggle their tails to draw small prey near.

heat-sensing pits

Copperheads have two **pits** on their heads that sense heat. The pits allow copperheads to find prey with a **body temperature** warmer than the air.

Copperheads bite their prey with sharp, curved **fangs**. A poison called **venom** flows through the fangs and into the bite.

fangs

The venom makes prey stop breathing and die. Copperheads then stretch their jaws wide and swallow their prey whole.

In winter, copperheads stop hunting. They **hibernate** with other snakes in a **den**. In spring, the hungry snakes come out to hunt again!

Glossary

body temperature—the amount of heat in an animal's body; a snake has a body temperature that is the same as its surroundings.

camouflage—coloring and patterns that hide an animal by making it look like its surroundings

den—a shelter where animals live or rest

fangs—sharp, curved teeth; copperheads have hollow fangs through which venom can move into a bite.

hibernate—to be inactive during winter; copperheads hibernate in dens with rattlesnakes, rat snakes, and other kinds of snakes.

pits—areas of a snake's face that sense the body heat of an animal; pits tell a snake where an animal is and how big it is.

poisonous—able to kill or harm with a poison; the venom that a copperhead makes is a poison.

predators—animals that hunt other animals for food

prey—animals hunted by other animals for food

scales—small plates of skin that cover and protect a snake's body

shed—to let something fall off; snakes rub their bodies against rocks or trees to help shed their skin.

snouts—the noses and jaws of animals

venom—a poison that some snakes make; copperhead venom is deadly.

To Learn More

AT THE LIBRARY

Gibbons, Gail. *Snakes*. New York, N.Y.: Holiday House, 2007.

Gunzi, Christiane. *The Best Book of Snakes*. New York, N.Y.: Kingfisher, 2003.

O'Hare, Ted. *Copperheads*. Vero Beach, Fla.: Rourke Publishing, 2005.

ON THE WEB

Learning more about copperheads is as easy as 1, 2, 3.

1. Go to www.factsurfer.com.

2. Enter "copperheads" into the search box.

3. Click the "Surf" button and you will see a list of related Web sites.

With factsurfer.com, finding more information is just a click away.

Index

The images in this book are reproduced through the courtesy of: Jill Cain, front cover; Jack Milchanowski/Photolibrary, pp. 4-5; Ryan M. Bolton, p. 6 (small); Jack Milchanowski/Age Fotostock, pp. 6-7, 8-9; Jim Merli/Getty Images, p. 9 (small); Jack Goldfarb/Photolibrary, p. 10; Todd Pusser/naturepl. com, p. 11; George Grall/Getty Images, pp. 12-13; Jon Eppard, pp. 13 (small), 16; Ronnie Howard, p. 14 (small); Heuclin Daniel/Age Fotostock, pp. 14-15; Kevin Messenger, p. 17; Frank Schneidermeyer/ Photolibrary, pp. 18-19; Kevin Fleming, p. 19 (small); Joe McDonald/Bruce Coleman Inc., p. 20; Mike VanValen, p. 21.